The Change in My Pocketbook

Why That "Secret Ingredient"
Always Seems Out of Reach

Lorene Collier Purcy

DEDICATION

To **all** those who inspired
my passion to be an entrepreneur!

CONTENTS

> A goal without a plan is just a wish.
>
> ~Larry Elder~

Whether you're a wannabe entrepreneur who is ready to take the plunge and start your own business, or you've been around the professional block a time or two already, there's one *"Secret Ingredient"* to your success that needs constant tending and updating. And that's your **GOALS.**

Everyone from Donald Trump to the eight-year-old with a lemonade stand has dreams and wishes. But until you put a timeline, milestones and measurements to your dream, you've got nothing – at least, nothing of value. Sure, a dream is a nice story to think about when you're falling asleep at night, but dreams don't get you bank loans, employees, or customers.

I wrote this book because I see too many business people of all levels getting stuck - not because they don't have good ideas; not because they lack motivation or smarts; not because they're won't roll up their sleeves, but because they simply don't have good, smart **GOALS.** They haven't set goals and designed strategies that will help them get from where they are today to where they're dreaming about being tomorrow. Often, the only difference between those who make it happen and those who don't make it happen is a person's willingness to set their goals. **Period.**

You wouldn't hire a contractor who didn't have a blueprint for your house. You wouldn't get on a plane with a pilot who didn't have an accurate navigational plan to where he was taking you. And you wouldn't want a barber who didn't know what your hair was supposed to look like when he was done cutting it. So why would you try to move forward in your business without concrete goals?

If you've never set specific goals before, or you've had trouble defining your goals in the past, never fear. Through this book, I'll share with you:

1. **why goals are important**

2. **what makes a good goal**

3. **how to keep on track, and**

4. **when to give up the ship.**

Now, let's get going...

Section 1 - Why Set Goals – Do Goals Matter?

> If you want to live a happy life, tie it to a goal, not to people or things.
>
> ~Albert Einstein~

Do goals matter? OF COURSE goals matter! That's the easy answer, but you didn't come here for the easy answer. You came here for a detailed step-by-step working strategy for setting and achieving your goals. So, let's look at specific reasons why goals matter.

Imagine you've been hired by NASA to get an astronaut into space. Now, "space" is an awfully big place. It might be a little more helpful if you had a tad more information about where exactly this astronaut was headed. The moon? An orbit around the earth? The space station? Without this data, you could easily spend years and millions of dollars executing a plan that misses the mark by a lot – oh, say, a few million miles.

When it comes to our businesses and personal lives, the risks may not be on quite so grand a scale, but they're very real to us. How will you develop a marketing plan to promote your latest product if you don't know how many you need to sell? How will you know whether you need new software for your network if you're not sure what you're trying to accomplish? How can you evaluate two possible courses of action if you don't know what the end goal is?

As it's been said in math classes since the beginning of time (almost), the straightest distance between two points is a straight line. But before you can create that line, you need the two points – a beginning (where you are now) and an end (your goal). Put simply, goals give you an endpoint. And once you have an endpoint, you can figure out how to get there – and evaluate the different plans and options before you.

Specifically, the benefits of goals include the following:

•Greater focus: Knowing your goals allows you to concentrate on your biggest priorities. When you're aware of your top goals, you can move them to the front of the line and stop worrying about the little things.

•Efficient allocation of resources: When you know what you're aiming for, you are less likely to waste time, money, or effort.

•Ability to measure progress: Goals make it easy to know if you're on the right path or not. You can easily measure your progress and determine how far off – or on – track you are. That's invaluable for making changes and adjustments along the way.

•Lower stress: Stress and anxiety often result from not knowing what you're supposed to be doing or where you should be concentrating your efforts. Goals lead to clarity of purpose, which leads to lower stress.

•Feelings of accomplishment: If you don't know where you're headed, you never know when you get there, and if you never know if you've arrived, you can never celebrate your success! Setting goals first allows you to know when you've done what you intended to do.

Now that you know why goals are important, let's talk about some of the biggest goal-setting mistakes people make.

Section 2 - How to Set Great Goals

A goal properly set is halfway reached.

~Abraham Lincoln~

Unfortunately, not every goal is a good goal. Goal-setting is a skill which can be broken down into three easily defined, concrete steps:

Brainstorm your big objective.

What are you trying to accomplish professionally or personally? Create a new product line? Cut costs? Streamline a process? Outsource some of your tasks? At this step, we're trying to get to your highest-level goal, so when you name something, ask yourself, "WHY?"

For instance, if you say, "I want to create a new

information product," then ask yourself, "Why?" You may answer, "So I can make money." That may seem like a logical endpoint, but don't stop there. You need to go further.

Ask yourself "WHY" you want to make money and you'll soon find out that there are a variety of possible motivators. You may hear yourself say something like this:

- I want to make more money so I can quit my day job.

- I want to make more money so I can take a vacation and pay cash.

- I want to make more money so I can pay off my debt.

- I want to make more money so I can buy a Maserati.

Each one of these higher-level objectives is slightly different, and is going to result in a slightly different goal or path to success. Knowing your "WHY" helps you determine your "HOW."

Define your goal in specific language.

It's not enough to know that you want to make money so you can quit your day job. In order to set an excellent goal, you need to know EXACTLY how much money you want to make.

Use losing weight as an example. Instead of the vague "I want to lose weight so I feel better," say, "I want to lose 20 pounds in six months so I can fit into my wedding dress (jeans, bathing suit, etc.)." The more specific and detailed you make your goal, the easier it is to visualize and measure your progress.

Here's another example. Let's say your goal is to outsource as much of your business as you can. Your "Why" is to save you time so you have the ability to create new products, so you can ultimately make more money and quit your day job. You may state a simple goal like "I want to outsource 50% of my tasks." Outsourcing is a worthy objective, but it's not a good goal. Because your real goal is to save time, you want to define your goal in terms of hours. A better goal would be, "I want to outsource enough work so I save myself 4 hours a day." This goal is much more defined and specific – and related to your higher-level objective!

Set a time-frame for your goal.

What if your goal was to make $10,000 to pay off your credit card debt. Do you want that money by next year? Or do you need it by the time you retire? What if you need it next month? Each of those scenarios will result in very different strategies.

Also, putting a time-frame to a goal gives it an inherent sense of urgency. As you know, many of us don't start working on a project until we have a deadline (and we wonder where our kids get it)! Even when a deadline is self-imposed, it helps motivate us.

Goal-setting isn't a scary, overwhelming, or extremely difficult task. In fact, it's pretty simple when you break it down into steps like this method illustrates. But it is still possible to make mistakes when creating and defining your goals. In the next section we're going to discuss mistakes in goal-setting, and what you can do to avoid them.

Section 3 - The Biggest Goal-Setting Mistakes and How to Overcome Them

The reason most people never reach their goals is that they don't define them, learn about them, or even seriously consider them as believable or achievable.

~Denis Waitley~

In my experience, these are the main reasons people make mistakes when setting their goals. Let's discuss each one in detail.

Not realistic.

Sometimes, you set goals that are perfectly reasonable – until you set a timeline on them. For instance, losing 20 pounds is great. Doing so by next Friday? Not so much.

I've found that, particularly with new entrepreneurs, the tendency is to overestimate the amount you can accomplish in a short period of time. Learning curves

– particularly online – can be steep, and unexpected obstacles arise. Then, when you face setbacks, you get discouraged and abandon the whole project because your original estimates weren't met.

Let me say this: things rarely go as planned – in business or in life. When setting your goals, build in some wiggle room that will allow you to handle unanticipated delays without throwing you totally off schedule. In other words, expect the unexpected and plan for it.

Not challenging enough.

The converse of the unrealistic goal is setting goals that aren't enough of a stretch. It may seem smart to set very low expectations, called "sandbagging" in the sales industry, but in actuality it can undermine your motivation. What's so great about running half a mile when you know you could easily run 10 times that much? Un-challenging goals are boring, too. It's hard to be proud of your accomplishments when you know you could have done much better.

Not specific.

If your goal is not specific enough, you're going to have trouble meeting it and being motivated by it. For instance, if your goal is a vague statement such as "lose weight," you could lose half a pound and call it a day. Is that satisfactory? Or, you could lose 20 pounds and feel disappointed. How do you know if you've achieved a goal if the goal is as vague as "lose weight?" If you're not feeling motivated by your goal, try making your goal more specific.

Not under your control.

Let's say you set a goal to publish a book with a major publisher. You wrote the manuscript, edited it, submitted it to an agent, got rejected, and submitted it to 20 more agents. And got rejected 20 more times. You felt like a complete failure because you hadn't met your goal of publishing a book.

The problem with this goal was that it was outside your control. You could set a goal about finishing and editing and submitting, but you couldn't count on an agent picking up your book, or a publisher finally publishing it. It was totally outside of your control! A better goal for you would have been "submit a complete manuscript to 20 agents this year." That goal you could control and enjoy a sense of accomplishment.

Not measurable.

Just like goals that aren't specific enough, goals that aren't measurable are impossible to meet. Let's say that your goal is to become a famous blogger. Great dream, but how will you measure that? You need an objective standard by which to measure your progress, and to tell if you've actually achieved your goal. If your goal isn't measurable, it isn't a good goal.

Not what you really wanted.

Let's say you set a specific goal that is measurable. You invest a lot of time and energy in your goal, and you do it! But instead of feeling like a million bucks, you're a little disappointed and lost. You said you wanted to create an affiliate program for your new product, and you did it – but why don't you feel like you've accomplished something? It could be because you set the wrong goal.

For example, look at the college grad that ends up in law school because her dad told her it was a good idea. Because she didn't have another goal or plan in mind, she finds herself falling into a plan she didn't want. Sometimes we fall into goals and hold onto them to the bitter end, treating our goals as if they were gospel.

Before you set a goal and dedicate resources towards its completion, make sure you've chosen the RIGHT goal. Use the "big objective" exercise in Section 2 to help you avoid this mistake.

You're now aware of the biggest pit-falls in goal-setting and how to avoid them. Next, let's talk about how to measure your progress.

Section 4 - Step by Step: Measuring Your Progress

Goals are dreams with deadlines.

~Diana Scharf Hunt~

Let's say you hop on a plane with your sweetie for a much-anticipated vacation in Bermuda. Your pilot gives you the standard greeting at take-off, and you enjoy the rest of the flight munching peanuts, watching a movie, and perusing overpriced merchandise in the in-flight magazine. Fifteen minutes before your scheduled landing, your pilot comes back on the intercom and says, "Umm... Sorry, folks. I forgot to check the navigation for the past few hours, so instead of landing in Bermuda, we'll be landing in Iceland."

Chances are you'd be less than thrilled. Why didn't the @#BLEEP!! pilot checks along the way to make sure you were headed in the right direction? Now you're going to have to spend your precious vacation time booking a flight out of Iceland!

Funny how ridiculous that sounds when applied to an airline. But many of us do the same thing with our business and personal goals all the time. We aim in the right direction, plug our noses, jump in, and then don't look up again until we either get there (by some stroke of luck) or we are so far off course that we have to call the Coast Guard to save us.

One of the most motivating – and overlooked – elements of goal-setting is measuring your progress. Measuring your success on a regular basis may sound like extra work, but, as our flight scenario illustrates, it has very real concrete advantages:

- Motivation: You're eager to continue when you see how much progress you're making.

- Course Correction: You can identify what's not working and make adjustments accordingly.

- Preservation of Resources: You can see where you're getting the biggest bang for your buck and save time, money, and effort.

In other words, a little effort in measurement will save you a ton of time, frustration, and money down the road.

Here's my three-step approach to measuring progress:

Step One: Define Your Units of Measure.

If you've set your goal to be specific and measurable, then it naturally must be measurable. The first step is to define your unit of measurement. If you want to lose weight, are you going to measure pounds lost, inches lost, or the size you can fit into? If you want to grow your business, are you going to measure the number of customers, the number of products released, or the dollars coming in the door? If you're having trouble deciding on units, return to your higher-level objective to see what your end desire is, and then select accordingly.

Step Two: Set Your Schedule.

Once you've decided on your units, determine how often you're going to measure your progress. Sometimes, more frequent measurement is better. But sometimes, checking in too frequently can actually discourage you. For instance, if you check your bank balance every half-hour and don't see any change, it can be de-motivating! Figure out a realistic amount of time, based on your goal and your units of measurement, to see some change. Then schedule those check-ins on your calendar.

Step Three: Evaluate.

On your appointed check-in times, do a brief evaluation of your progress. Get on your scale, check your debt pay-down, and look at your customer list.

Then ask yourself if you're making the progress you need to get the results you want. If so, wonderful! If not, why not? If you haven't lost an ounce, have you been changing your behavior to be more active and eat better? If you haven't gained any customers, have you been advertising, marketing, or looking for joint venture partners?

Evaluating what you've done, or perhaps what you HAVEN'T done, will give you a good idea of what's working and what's not. Evaluating your progress will get and keep you motivated because you'll actually be paying attention to the fruits of your labor.

If you've been taking the right steps, but aren't seeing the results you desire, keep reading. It may be a matter of haven chosen the wrong goals.

Section 5 - When to Adapt and Change Your Goals

You must have long term goals to keep you from being frustrated by short term failures.

~Charles C. Noble~

Sometimes, you feel like you're doing all the right things, but you're not getting anywhere. If you truly are putting in the effort and following the strategy outlined so far, it may be a matter of choosing the wrong goals. Let's see if it's time to change your goals:

The situation has changed.

Let's say your goal is to sell 1000 copies of a new information product called, "Developing Applications for the iPhone 2G." The day after you start writing, Apple releases a new version of the iPhone, the 3G. Suddenly, the scenario has changed. Developers aren't looking to create applications for the iPhone 2G anymore. Customers are in line at the Apple store now trading in their 2Gs for a 3G. Your market just evaporated overnight. You could write and release the best book under the sun and no one would buy it because it's obsolete.

If the business environment has changed, then your goals may have to change, too.

Your priorities have changed.

Maybe you're making great progress towards your goals, but you suddenly realize what you thought was really important, such as losing weight, is less important than helping your child improve his math skills, or taking a family vacation, or spending more hours to get your new business off the ground.

If your priorities have changed, it's time to take a look at your goals.

Your higher-level objective has changed.

You thought you wanted to make more money so you could save for retirement, but your son just got invited to attend an elite soccer clinic this summer, with an elite price tag. Suddenly, you need that extra cash NOW.

You may have to adjust your goals to match your new higher-level objectives.

Your goal wasn't the right one to begin with.

As we discussed in a previous section, you can make great progress towards your goal if you follow the right strategies... but towards the wrong goal! When setting goals, you have to ensure that the higher-level objective and the goal itself fit with your desires, ethics, and personal style. Your goal may be a mismatch.

You may have to revisit the goal setting process outlined in Section 2 to see if the goal is right for you.

Your resources have changed.

When we select a goal and a path for getting there, we make certain assumptions. We typically assume we'll have a certain amount of time, energy, and money to dedicate to the completion of the goal. For instance, if you are working to expand into a new market, you might set a goal of creating and releasing one email marketing message and video per week. Then you get word that your main product line is facing threats from a competitor's marketing efforts. You may have to take resources from the new goal to shore up the marketing for your main product line. Your new marketing goal has to change in order to reallocate resources to your main business.

If your anticipated resources must be redirected or

become depleted, you may have to change your goal as well.

Sometimes, as we've seen, you do need to take another look at your goals to make sure they still fit your overall objectives, resources, and priorities. But most of the time, when you plan carefully for your new goal, you'll be able to carry on toward completion. The next section will share some surefire methods for achieving those goals.

Section 6 - Surefire Strategies to Achieve Your Goals

Our goals can only be reached through a vehicle of a plan, in which we must fervently believe, and upon which we must vigorously act. There is no other route to success.

~Stephen A. Brennan~

Even when you've set a "good" goal - one that adheres to your higher objective and is specific and measurable - you can run into some issues along the way... namely, motivation. Without motivation, even the most ambitious person will get sidetracked. Here are the strategies that will keep you on track to achieving your goals:

Get a buddy.

Life can be lonely when you are making changes to your behavior. Your friends, family, and work colleagues may not support "the new you." For instance, if you're trying to start a new business, your spouse may not "get" it and may question the time that you devote towards your goal. Having a buddy or accountability partner to constantly check in with and rely on for support can be invaluable.

The best partners are those who are undertaking the same process, or have walked the same path before. Find someone who will help you identify obstacles, provide advice, and cheer you on through the process of achieving your goal. Support is key to your goal's success.

Focus on success.

Getting waylaid by negative thoughts or "what if" scenarios can spell disaster, even death, to your goals. When you start out by finding a million ways why your plans won't work, your energy is getting diverted to dealing with failure that hasn't even happened!

Instead of funneling your time and resources into negative thoughts and processes, make the decision that you're not going to entertain any ideas of failure. If it happens, it happens. You don't have to spend your precious resources worrying about it now.

Donald Trump is famous for his positive attitude. Even when he was in debt to the tune of billions (yes, BILLIONS!) of dollars, he rallied his team with pictures of the deals they would make in the future. His energy was contagious, and he was able to pull himself and his company out of bankruptcy with the help of focusing on forthcoming success.

Make it public.

You know why shows like "Biggest Loser" work? Because no one wants to admit they wimped out on their diet or skipped their 6 AM gym appointment in front of millions of viewers! The "Biggest Loser" contestants have the ultimate motivation – a camera in their face 24/7.

While you may not want to keep a camera on you 'round the clock, you will want to make your goal public. Tell your friends, family, colleagues, and even the internet on forums, websites, or your blog. It works!

Chart your progress.

I've already shared with you the importance of measuring your progress. A great motivation is to create a visual graphic to represent your progress towards your goal. Think of those thermometers that elementary schools place outside on a busy road, measuring how close they are to achieving their fund-raising goal for the new community pool or library. A similar, physical chart that you can update with progress will do wonders to keep your attention focused.

When you're doing this step, think outside the box. If

you're trying to spend more time at the gym, why not post a map of the US on your wall, and draw an inch from one coast to the other for each hour you spend on the treadmill? If you're increasing your income, place a penny in a jar on your desk for each $10 or $100 you earn. These visual reminders are fun ways to keep your goals in the forefront of your mind.

Turn to an expert for advice.

We often think we need to do everything on our own. Nothing could be further from the truth! Alcoholics Anonymous has sponsors, Michael Phelps has a coach, and Jack Welch had an advisory board. No one has to be alone in their goal-setting efforts. Trying to eat healthier? Nutritionists will help you fine-tune your diet. Working out to get fit? Trainers will help you find the most effective exercises to achieve your physical goals.

There are business mentors and coaches who can help you figure out social media, launch a new information product, or streamline your finances. You can also find tons of books, videos, and websites to help you reach your goal, no matter what your goal happens to be. Don't go it alone. Someone else has already invented that wheel and is ready to help you use it!

Now that your motivation is revved up, let's take a look at how to rein in that energy to keep you focused and on task.

Section 7 - Tried-and-True Methods to Stay Focused

Set your goals high, and don't stop till you get there.

~Bo Jackson~

Got your goals set and your motivation and systems in place? Great! Now let's talk about keeping focused.

Focus is a problem even for the most energetic goal-setter. In fact, it's often more likely that people with the most energy have the least focus. If you've been blessed with an extra helping of "Just Do It," read this section carefully! Getting distracted is one of the biggest problems in goal achievement, particularly with longer-term goals. Use these methods to keep your head down and your eye on the prize:

Commit.

This may sound a bit silly since you've already been through the goal-setting stage. Shouldn't that mean you're already committed? But, some people who are really good at setting goals and getting started; forget that they actually have to show up, day-in and day-out, until the goal is reached. That's why I recommend having a little heart-to-heart with yourself in which you think through your "why" and restate your commitment to doing what it takes to "get 'er done."

Think of standing at the altar with your beloved and going through the marriage ceremony, including the "'til death do us part" section. You may be in love with that person and want to create a fabulous future together, but until you make that official commitment, your dedication may be a bit lacking. Commit to your goal the way you'd commit to a partner.

Slow down.

If you're a natural go-getter, you can be a bit of a loose cannon doing a lot of "stuff" but not necessarily doing the RIGHT stuff. As a result, you spin your wheels at times, wasting energy on tasks that aren't directly contributing to your ultimate goal, and starting new "projects" in the process. Often I am approached by new entrepreneurs who excitedly rattle off a list of ten new projects and ask me if they are good ideas. The answer is "yes" ten times; "but now pick one and stick to it until it's done."

In other words - Slow Down! Before you take on any additional project or responsibility, ask yourself how it's going to affect your ability to devote needed resources towards your current goals. Before you start anything else, ask yourself if you wouldn't be better off sticking with the pile of goals that are already partly completed. Take a deep breath and try to be a little more Zen. Your slow and steady pace will pay off when you save yourself from burn-out.

Don't expect immediate payoff.

As I mentioned above, those of you blessed with a great deal of energy may have what's known as "entrepreneurial ADD." You try something, it works for a little bit, and then it gets kind of boring, or the original results start to trail off. That's when you switch and try something else. You repeat the process until you have a shelf full of diet books or a computer hard drive full of half-finished projects. Stop!

Success comes not from the first five sit-ups you do in your workout today, but from the last five sit-ups you squeak out at the end of your workout. You know the ones you do when you think you're too tired to do any more.

Likewise, success comes from the last five emails you force yourself to send, or the last five cold calls you make after everyone else has gone home for the day. Aim to push yourself to the edge – and then go a little further. Results take time.

Set aside some time each day.

If you tend to be a "starter" rather than a "finisher," you may need more structure to your time. One technique for staying the course is to set aside a specific amount of time each day to focus on your goals - AND ONLY your goals. That means no checking email, no combing the dog, and no phone calls.

Time set aside for your goals could be as little as fifteen minutes or as long as an hour. What matters is making this time that you set aside become a habit; this is the time you "punch in" each and every day to work on your long-term projects. This discipline will move you forward, bit by bit, if you are consistent.

Reward yourself for focus, not just for accomplishments.

While it's great to have rewards in place for when you achieve your goals, it's important for those of us who tend to fall off-task to reward ourselves for effort and focus, not just our accomplishments.

Rewards for focusing on our goals don't have to be big or expensive. They could be as simple as saying to yourself, "I'll check email after I finish writing this chapter," or, "I'll go for coffee when I've finished reviewing the product launch schedule." It really works! I know because I use this technique all the time. In fact, I'm going to go relax and watch "The Office" right after I finish this section. Good job, me!

Okay, now we're really on our way! Let's take a look at how you can use technology to help achieve your goals.

Section 8 - Using Technology to Support Your Goals

Progress has little to do with speed, but much to do with direction.

~Anonymous~

Technology – everything from our computer to our cell phone – seems to have invaded every area of our modern lives. But we often under-use technology, not taking full advantage of the features and benefits that can really make our lives easier. Here's how you can leverage the technology you already have to help you achieve your goals:

Set alarms.

Use the alarms on your computer or cell phones to keep you on task and concentrating for specific time periods. There are many free programs available that allow you to set alarms and timers right on your computer. Haven't set up a program like that for yourself yet? Go get the trusty kitchen timer and get back to work!

Track your hours.

Want to know how much time you're REALLY wasting on activities like email, online shopping, and Farmville? Use an online service like RescueTime.com to track time on different activities. You'll be surprised at the end of the day how much time you spend on non-productive activities when you're not paying attention. Aside from keeping you honest about how much time you waste, if you flip between two or three real projects during the day, with a program like this, you'll be able to see where your focus has been on those projects. So even time well-spent can be tracked for the purpose of staying ON track.

Join a group.

Join a forum or email list of people who are working on similar goals as you are. Do a search at Groups.Google.com or Groups.Yahoo.com to find email lists on literally thousands of topics. Whether you're starting a company, founding a non-profit, trying to lose weight, or writing a book, you'll find a group that's right for you. Now, be careful. You don't want these groups or forums to take your focus away from your daily tasks and goals. But the information and support of a group of like-minded individuals can be invaluable.

Track your progress.

Use Excel's charting option to create an ongoing chart or graph of your progress. Print it out or use it as your screen-saver for extra motivation. As we discussed, accurate measurements as we move along toward our goals is crucial. Simply jotting down this measured progress in notebooks is fine, but why not use technology to expand your knowledge, tweaking data to give you even more information.

Set reminders.

You can set reminder emails on your computer or calls on your cell phone. When the email or call comes in, you know it's time to go for your run, sit down for a planning session, or perform the next step on your list. Don't try to keep your schedule in your brain. Let technology do it for you and free up your brain cells for the real work... achieving your goals!

Brainstorm.

Mind mapping software like FreeMind, MindGenius, MindManager, VisualMind, and VUE allow you to brainstorm and capture your ideas in a visual format. Mind mapping is a great way to figure out steps towards a goal, determine priorities, and even write blog posts, books, and more. There are plenty of brain-flexing capabilities programmed into this software, so have fun with it. Explore your thoughts right there on your computer screen.

Find mentors.

Whether you need someone to take a look at your business plan or help you figure out the tax implications of hiring off-shore workers, you can find great mentors in every field. Ask successful colleagues to drop a few names or do a quick Google search to look at the options available. The thing to remember is someone has done it before – whatever it is – and is very often pleased to assist someone just starting out with the same goal.

Network.

As I mentioned earlier, working on new projects can be lonely, particularly when you're stretching yourself outside your current comfort zones. Even if you're not looking for an accountability partner right now, you can still network with others in the same industry, sharing resources and war stories. Or just vent – that's important, too!

Get training.

One of the first places I look when I'm trying to figure something out is YouTube. There are tens of thousands of videos created for everything from the proper form for push-ups to how to install a WordPress blog. Before you go and pay someone to help you learn something, do a quick search and see if you can find the information and figure out what you need to know – with a little help from your YouTube friends.

Create an informal focus group.

Want a quick weigh-in on whether Logo #1 or Logo #2 better expresses your company's brand? Need to know if stay-at-home moms respond to headlines the way you hope they will? Looking for the best music to run to? Log onto Twitter or Facebook and ask away. Within minutes you'll have tons of answers – for free! You won't have to get stuck waiting for feedback before you can move on. Wham, bam, and you're back in business.

Blog your experiences.

Everyone loves a good success story, particularly one from an "ordinary" person. And, everyone loves to share their own experiences when asked. Start a blog and create an online journal of your journey towards your goal. Not only will you have the motivation of knowing your blog readers are following your efforts, you will most likely get feedback from your readers that will trigger all sorts of new ideas - you just might have an information product in the making.

Ask for support.

Every once in a while, you may need an impromptu cheering section. Facebook, Twitter, and other social media outlets are perfect for that very thing. Let your followers know when you just need to hear a "You can do it!" You'll be surprised at how many people have walked in your shoes and are happy to chime in and give you a thumbs-up, at-a-boy, or at-a-girl.

By now, you're a goal-setting expert! But even when you do everything right, there are times when things aren't working out the way you'd planned. That's why the next section teaches you how to handle "failure."

Section 9 - What to Do if You "Fail?"

Success is not final, failure is not fatal: it is the courage to continue that counts.

~Winston Churchill~

I have put the word "fail" in quotes in the title because I strongly believe that you never REALLY fail if you've learned something. There's a difference between a good goal and a good outcome – sometimes, despite your best efforts, you can't make even a good goal work.

In my experience, there are three main reasons for "failure:"

Your goal was wrong.

You did all the right things, but you were aiming at the wrong target. For instance, let's say you wanted to do something to help people (your higher-level objective) so you decided to go to law school (your goal). Unfortunately, you can't stand to study, read, or write. And you hate being in conflict with people! There's an inherent mismatch between your personality and the goal you chose.

Have you "failed?" No. Your goal was wrong. You may have spent time and money that you'd rather not have spent, but think about what you learned: You are a doer, not a studier. Yes, you still want to help people, but now you know you want to do so in a more collegial fashion.

That's great information to know about yourself. Many people don't find out what they really want to do with their lives until they're in the corner suite, and miserable! Treat this setback as a valuable learning experience. Spend time thinking about the lessons you've learned and how you can avoid making the same mistake next time. Then, as the song goes, "pick yourself up, dust yourself off, and start all over again."

Your path was wrong.

Sometimes you have a great goal, but you just pick the wrong path for getting there. That's like knowing where you want to go on the other side of town, but picking the road that's under construction, full of detours, and jammed with bumper-to-bumper traffic. There's nothing wrong with your goal; you just picked a lousy route.

To bring this into the business realm, it would be a case of knowing what result you want (let's say, more sales) but choosing a strategy that doesn't pay off (advertising at bus stops when your target customer has a chauffeur).

Sometimes you don't know you've chosen the wrong path until you're halfway down the road. This is a major bummer – you've invested a lot of time and money and suddenly, wham! There's that detour sign. You then have a choice – do you suck it up and keep going, hoping it will get better? Or do you cut your losses, backtrack, and start over again?

As much as you hate to hear it, you're usually better off heading back to the "Go" square and starting out with a fresh start. If this makes you cringe, let me tell you a story. Maxine Hong Kingston, the fabulous novelist, had almost finished a manuscript for a new book, "The Fourth Book of Peace." It was completely destroyed in the Oakland fires of 1991. Kingston went on to write a new book, "The Fifth Book of Peace," which included a rewritten version of the destroyed book. Now that is "rising from the ashes"... literally.

If you need to start over, glean the best of what went right before and add it to your knowledge banks. Then set the past aside and get crackin'!

Your execution was wrong.

The goal was right. The path was right. But, your execution? Not so much. Maybe your motivation started flagging. Maybe you started cutting corners.

Or maybe you just gave up. Whatever the reason, the result was the same: Your goal remains out of reach.

If the reason for your "failure" lies at your feet, take a look at your motivation. Why did it drop? Did you try all the strategies in Section 6? Are you still committed to this goal? Do you need additional resources? Figure out where the disconnect is, then try, try again.

"Failure" to me is just another word for "Things didn't turn out quite like I had planned." There are still plenty of lessons to be learned – sometimes more so than if everything had panned out just right. This next section will show you that sometimes it may be time to just let your goal go – for good reason.

Section 10 - When to Give Up on Your Goals

When it is obvious that the goals cannot be reached, don't adjust the goals, adjust the action steps.

~Confucius~

Giving up sounds so negative. But can you make room in your brain for the possibility that you can release your goals without being a failure? It's true. Sometimes the goals themselves are unreachable, for no reason you can control. There are times to let your goal go – or at least set it aside for a while. Here are some of those times:

You just can't get motivated.

Have you ever made plans to go to a movie with a friend or attend a party, but when it came time to get ready to go, you just couldn't get going? Maybe you decided you didn't really want to see that show, or you're having a grand old time just sitting on the couch in your sweats with a pint of Ben & Jerry's. But, whatever the reason, the motivation is just not there.

If you've tried all the suggestions in Section 6 and Section 7, and you keep missing deadlines, failing to take the next step, or simply not acting on your goal, it may be time to let that goal go, at least for now. Sometimes it's a disconnect you haven't been able to pinpoint, or sometimes the timing's just not right. It's okay to just set the goal aside and move on to something more attractive. No one's keeping score – I promise.

You don't know what to do next.

If you are lost, unsure which direction to go in next, which path to take, or what you really want, it may be time to stop striving. Instead of feeling like you HAVE to have a goal, take some time to reflect and figure out what you're really trying to achieve with your business or your life.

Though I'm all in favor of action, I think it's much smarter to make sure you're choosing the right goal and the right strategies, rather than just acting for the sake of acting. You can't get where you want to go until you know where it is you want to go! Simple enough.

You are exhausted.

Type-A, ultra-motivated goal-setters can burn themselves out pretty quickly. It's hard to stay motivated if you never give yourself recovery time, instead bouncing from one huge project to the next. It won't matter how successful you are if you don't have the energy, or give yourself the time, to enjoy your achievements.

If you're bordering on burnout, give yourself a break. Set all your goals aside for a while and just relax. It'll pay off in the long run.

You've changed your mind.

Contrary to popular belief, it is okay to change your mind. You may be halfway to a goal, or even closer, and decide it's a bad idea or it's just not a goal that you long for anymore. That's okay. Really.

If you think you've changed your mind about a goal, take time to ask yourself "why." Is it a higher-level objective issue? A strategy issue? Or are you just not sure? Figure out how you feel about your goal before you decide to let it go. If after you've explored your "why" and your feelings about your goal, you decide letting go of your goal is the right thing for you right now, release it and move on. No regrets – just lessons learned.

As a final thought on this topic, I can't resist putting in this quote for obvious reasons:

"The only thing you live to regret are the risks you didn't take." ~Anonymous~

Conclusion

The major reason for setting a goal is for what it makes of you to accomplish it. What it makes of you will always be the far greater value than what you get. ~Jim Rohn~

By working your way through this book, you should now be in a much better position to set your goals and achieve them – even take the world by storm!

Whether you're hoping to remodel your home, self-publish a book of business lessons, lose weight, or find your ideal job, you've got the tools now to help you identify and achieve your goals... yes, even your dreams.

I look forward to seeing your successes in the future. Thank you for allowing me the privilege of being part of your journey.

About the Author

Lorene Collier Purcy is known for a contagious

passion for excellence, a talent for practical business solutions, and a competence for being a motivational leader. She is an international author, professional speaker, business adviser and life prosperity coach. She is also the President & CEO The SAVVY Consultant a coaching and consulting company for entrepreneurs, independent professionals and small business owners.

The Savvy Consultant is a boutique small business coaching and consulting firm focused on helping the small business owner develop effective cash flow strategies and business development processes.

Lorene coauthored (3) books "The Power of Change: Reinventing Yourself at Any Age", "How to Break the Glass Ceiling Without a Hammer: Career Strategies for Women" and "Ready, Aim, Soar" along with dozens of eBooks and articles.

Visit www.thesavvyconsultant.com to **download FREE goal setting worksheet** and learn more key strategies on how to start, expand or grow your business and keep your cash flowing in the right direction.

www.ingramcontent.com/pod-product-compliance
Lightning Source LLC
Chambersburg PA
CBHW071643170526
45166CB00003B/1416